Ends Are Beginnings

Ends Are Beginnings

Sangeeta Gupta

Prithvi Fine Art and Cultural Centre,
A1/232, Safdarjung Enclave,
New Delhi-110029

ISBN : 978-81-950284-2-9

Ends Are Beginnings
Poems by Sangeeta gupta

Paperback edition 2020

Cover Painting : Sangeeta Gupta

Price : ₹ 99.00

Printer:
Colour Bussiness Centre
75, Jain Mandir Marg, Sector-4, Gole
Market, New Delhi-110001

*For
All caterpillars
who dare to
transform
into butterflies.*

Contents

Ends Are Beginnings 1

Butterfly is born
when a caterpillar
comes out of its comfort zone
dares to take
the path less travelled
unknown, uncertain
It's her love for life...
she dares to
kill herself for passion
goes through the turmoil
the toil, sweat and
anxiety of becoming
the journey long and lonesome
has died a thousand death
to be, to live
never gave up
went all the way to become
your love, hatred or indifference
doesn't affect her a bit
she loves herself enough
don't envy the butterfly
salute her indomitable spirit
butterfly is born
when a caterpillar
comes out of its comfort zone.

Ends Are Beginnings 2

Outgrowing
your thoughts
your way of living
outgrowing people
once dear to you
rejecting your past no way
your journey it is
travel back ever
not possible
cling to the known
live in your comfort zone forever
not a choice
one and only reference point
is your connect
with the universe
the only eternal truth
to move on towards
your better version
you realise
that you have
outgrown yourself
it is the end
a beginning as well
you are reborn
not knowing the next step
not sure of the next breath
is the miracle called life
you move with
your trust and love for life
outgrowing yourself
is your faith in life.

An Ode To Van Gogh

Van Gogh's yellow dazzles
my dream
and suddenly I wake up to
a bright day
sunflowers singing
straight from his paintings
fill my heart with unknown joy
his starry nights
fill my darkness
I walk with dancing lights
I wake up from my dream
lying still in the midnight
burst into tears
of intense passion
for his lust for life
Van Gogh's yellow dazzles
my dream...

Artists Think

Artists think
they choose the colour
it is not the truth
colour chooses the artist
one cannot choose
to be an artist
cannot desire or
want to be an artist
you become an artist
because art chose you
consumed by the passion
you go all the way
till you become one with art
there is no other way to become.

My Bed

My bed...
the creative zone
of this day dreamer
lazy poet
who lived in her own world
of books and more books
and few dreams
not a morning person
loved sleeping more than
anything else
fragile, fussy about food
shy, introvert
never wished to annoy a soul
a bundle of all that
my father didn't approve
he failed to
discipline me
he thought I was the rebel
without a cause
understand he didn't
the becoming of a lazy poet
I didn't choose to be a poet
poetry chose me
it came to me
I didn't try to be a poet
poetry came to me as a twin soul.

A Blank Paper Or Canvas

*A blank paper or canvas
is so enticing
they are my muse
their endearing charm
is mesmeric
I can't escape
I throw my whole persona
on them
oblivious of the outcome
I pour my heart and soul
soiled in ink or colours
we become inseparable
I die a thousand deaths
they convert me
into an energy field
we are born in unison then.*

Poetry For Me

Poetry for me is not
the conscience keeper
It is my journal of
inner dialogue
which happens
between me and life
between me and you
what remains unsaid
you never had the time
nor the much needed space
it is a narrative of
sustained pain
of not being loved
or understood
failures and triumphs
narrative of an intimate journey
private yet intensely passionate
from known to uncertain
from logic to beyond logic
from darkness to light
poetry for me is not
the conscience keeper.

If You Cannot Be A Poet

If you cannot be a poet,
be a poem
you decided to be the poem
and I the poet.
all your telepathic thoughts
touched my soul
and became poems
on my lonesome path
nothing seemed to be known
nothing seemed to be certain
I cling to you my poems
these were not mere words
they were my little tiny candles
in the darkest of nights
I walked in the storm
by myself
I cling to you my poems
and the journey from
nothing to nothing
became so worthwhile.
If you cannot be a poet,
be a poem
you decided to be the poem
and I the poet.

I Keep You As A Poem

I keep you as a poem
in the core of my existence
I sing all day
you my song
you often shine as the evening star
in my lonesome dreams
you hold my hand
when I am lost in the wilderness
you, the lifeline of a poet
I keep you as a poem
in the core of my existence.

Do You Realise

*Do you realise
how often you
walk in
in my poems
you sit there
like a baby
till I hug you
express you
on a piece of my soul
there is no space for pain or joy
my soul is so, so filled with you
I am amazed
you still want more of my soul
and incessantly
you create eternal spaces
in my core existence
for yourself
do you realise
how often you
walk in
in my poems.*

Let A Poem Be

Let a poem be
a shelter for lonesome
tired souls
devoid of love and light
let them sit with a poem
and sip life
do nothing, kill time
whatever they wish
and move on
with energy.

When The Boatman

*When the boatman
sings to the river
river laughingly
sings back to him
river songs of
forgotten civilisations
songs of untold stories
of hearts broken on its banks
songs of hope and despair
I sit down in my solitude
lost to the world
I hear quietly
all these songs
of the river
of the boatman
and then I too sing
to you my soul
in utter silence
burning the mid night lamp
wide awake yet not restless ever
songs which are yet to be born
songs which I will never
be able to sing
to you my soul.*

Learn To Love The Darkness

Learn to love the darkness
deep dark night is the only refuge
where you cannot see,
however hard you try
then the only choice left is
to give up on seeing
and only then
you start to feel
feel your own body, your soul
you realise you cannot brush aside
so much of raw, intense passion
you know how vulnerable
how sensitive
you are within
you suddenly see
after a while you can
actually see in the dark
your whole being
engulfed in love
never expressed
your core so pure, untouched
you stop judging yourself
like everyone does
around your little world
you realise how worthless all your pursuits
have been
worldly success is so futile
when you have not
loved beyond reason
and you have not been
loved without reason

In the darkness
you weep your heart out
you have never felt so utterly lonely
you are lost to existence
it is alright, no worries
you can cry in the darkness
nobody is watching.
the only solace is
now you know
who you are
not the one you smile at
in the mirror of your bathroom
each morning
you met your real self
in the deep dark night
learn to love the darkness.

Life

Life
I am not done yet
don't give up on me
bit by bit I pull myself
from my ashes
like a phoenix
I rise to read my poems to you
they narrate your little nothings
the sheer joy of being alive still
is your greatest gift
in deep meditation
in intense silence
I offer you a song
as my prayer
Life
I am not done yet
don't give up on me
bit by bit I pull myself
from my ashes
like a phoenix.

Rebel Against Whom

Rebel against whom
I rebel against my old patterns
my obsessions
my commitments to non essentials
I now commit to myself first
I now love myself first
I am kind to myself
I fill myself with life.

What No Longer Serves Us

What no longer serves us
be done away with
people outgrow people
and move on
it hurts those
who still can't think of
having a life without the one
who has outgrown you
it's your problem
learn to let go of the one
who is no more yours
not easy
but let go
liberate the one who is gone
in the process
you will liberate yourself.

Days Of Emptiness

Days of emptiness
are not forced on me
It is a conscious decision
to empty myself
of all non essentials
cluttered
during my journey so far
on this planet earth
incessant movement of life
is the only movement in my life now
I have surrendered
myself to life.
I have always loved life
I love it more than ever
now I do not seek anything
I have given up
on planning my life
no goals, no targets
I trust life
I let it happen to me.

All Said And Done

All said and done
One cannot
do away with the past completely
memories come back often
anxious moments
about future also mingle with the present
the only endeavour of a living being
is to be aware of it
and come back
to the present moment
as fast as one can
present is always loaded
with past baggage
images of an unknown future
also cannot be shun away
though one must attempt
to hold the moment tight
in an intense embrace.

Ah Ha Moment

*Ah ha moment is
being more in the moment
than over obsessing
with the past or future
release unhealthy dynamic
of being over involved
in others life
overcome co dependents
it is a personal detriment
fast track desire
to be centered
and more whole
love yourself enough
to regain self esteem.*

You Allow

You allow
time to watch you
you put in herculean effort
to do nothing and get tired
except
let time soak in your being
trying to know you
you are a mere silent spectator
letting time to understand you
you who never had time
now sits idle, do nothing
just allow time to sit by you
while you drink
your morning cup of tea
it is not your intention to escape
from life
or escape from love
but you want to be yourself
not lost to love
not lost to pain.
you wish to
just be
you allow
time to watch you.

All Doors

All doors
are meant to be closed
at some point of time
windows are meant
to open
and inspire us
to look out
for life
life is born each day
hold it tight
until the next day
I look for a window
to find life.

I like the way life

*I like the way life
is unfolding itself to me
there is a magical bonding
between us
I trust the unknown
I love the uncertain
it is devoid of stress
there is no burden to perform
I let go of plans
there are no goals
losing control was
not easy for this workhorse
but now I have learnt this art
It is fun to be friends with life
I let life take charge of me
I let life happen to me.*

I Empty Myself Ruthlessly

I empty myself ruthlessly
nothing, absolutely nothing
is left in me
I then walk inside
I go into myself
I fill myself with
myself
I grope inside as deep as I can
I discover myself
connected to the source.

I Am A Free

I am a free,
passionate,
creative spirit
only love can bind me
I belong to life
I love freedom
I love my solitude
I love life
let life love me
and bind me
in solitude
in freedom.

May Be

May be
more than love
we need compassion
a smile
to survive the storm
an act of kindness
like just holding the hand
of a fellow traveller on this planet
sometimes is more than enough
one can heal
the curse of a lifetime
with a comforting touch
all one needs in a crisis is
a word of solace
I know all of this
because of the storm
I faced and survived.

Santa Claus Be

Santa Claus be
our role model
not just for Christmas
but for keeps.
for sharing
tangible intangible
abstract gift of love
keep hearts warm
Santa adds
beauty to the world so mundane
gift of love
is what we crave for

Deep Listening

Deep listening
devoid of
any urge to speak
or need to interrupt
relieves the pain
of the speaking soul
filled with anguish and grief
that is an act of pure love
and compassion
learn to listen
learn to love.

Life Is Available Only

Life is available only
in here and now
our true home it is
in the process of becoming
I slow down
poise
become still
float in timelessness
create space for spaceless
silence surrounds me
almost audible
subconscious hurts heal
scared child within liberates
deeply empowering experience it is
how difficult it is to be simple

Wandering In Wilderness

Wandering in wilderness
is romancing with life
travelling by yourself
is fun if you
love your company
nothing on my mind
nothing to plan or structure
is slowing down
relaxing and accepting
all that is going to unfold
I allow life to be, to do nothing
storms come and go
and come back yet again
I am just a witness
to all that happens
or happens not.
now I have learned
to trust life and let it live.

Break The Spell Of Mundane

*Break the spell of mundane
everyday distractions
to do away with them
needs your will
heal the wounded child within
release pent up
emotional stress forever
stop recycling
painful patterns and beliefs
hiding behind
the smaller version of your self
will not help
Inner working on self love is a process
engage in it whole heartedly
let your true self
shine unapologetically.*

Words May Not Reach

Words may not reach
how about thoughts
can one block
can one delete
like unstoppable sea
will flow thoughts
they will reach you
they will reach me
can we escape from thoughts
denial of passion
hits one more
than its acceptance
accept to heal thy self
let love liberate.

Let Go Of The Past

Let go of the past
move on with life
I can never say so
there is so much valuable
so,so precious about one's past
there are those sweet little memories
I treat them
as my inheritance
my heritage
I preserve them
in my museum of memories.
they will be treasured
till I breathe my last
all of past was not waste
not all of it was mundane
I often visit
my museum of memories
return fully charged
to love a new day
with a poem in my heart.

Silence Has The Grace

Silence has the grace
of a beautiful breeze
at the day break
so pure
devoid of any violence
yet so potent
a defence without offence
silence is intense
deeply moving
unsung soul song
words always engage one
invariably provoke to respond
they intimidate
force one to communicate
words break
the magical spell of silence
silence demands nothing
profound and liberating it is
seeks only understanding
silence has the grace of
a beautiful breeze
at the day break.

Every Death Reminds Us

*Every death reminds us
of our own fate
we mourn
not the departed
we mourn
our own mortality
death is mere reminder
of uncertain life
stay alive till the end
death is a season
and so is life
we mortals are aware
but never accept.*

Life Is A Charisma

Life is a charisma
a flowing river of eternity
as if never going to cease
life doesn't accept death
as its end
how lesser mortals
then can accept death
as end inevitable
Life is a charisma
a flowing river of eternity.

To Return Back In Time

To return back in time
or space
not possible
 not even an option
one cannot embrace
the same moment ever
you return back
to memories
life, time and space
all move on
love dies every night
to be born
with the sun in the morn
yet one craves
for all that is gone
oblivious of
what one has.

Life Says

Life says
don't die before your time
come hold me in a tight hug
I am all yours
before you go back
I love you anyway
so live me to the fullest
here and now.

Man Himself

Man himself
is the real danger
to save humanity
we humans
need to understand
the psyche of humans
more than ever before
humans not animals
are destroying nature
only humans are capable
of destroying humans
mysteries of human mind
be understood better
for our own survival
Carl Gustav Jung
the psychoanalyst said so
time and again
man himself
is the real danger.

In This Era Of Darkness

In this era of darkness
learning to deal with
our own darkness
is the only way to deal with it
walk, walk all the way
in isolation
learn to love solitude
at the edge of nowhere
somewhere there is magic
there is light
go all the way
know that
have faith
you are bound to discover it
treasure of abundant light
is to be shared
with some lonesome
that is all one can do
In this era of darkness.

Love Is The Only Way

Instantaneous pleasures
torment one
soon after the ecstatic temporary highs
with soul crushing lows
profound inner shift
only can bring
a sense of groundedness
grips of debilitating insecurity
can only subside
with outpouring of gratitude
learn to love yourself
with no ifs no buts
love is the only way
to reach Him
your purpose.

It Is More Fictional Than Real

It is more fictional than real
in a moment of deep despair
a soul seeks out
for help
and finds a twin soul
they were bound to meet
but they are oblivious
of their karmic connection
of many lives
they part
and yet are inseparable
there is magic between the two
they bring emotional satisfaction
to each other
they feel
they understand
without words
it is a miracle
it is more fictional than real.

Some Souls

Some souls
fill in
your empty existence
and only then it sinks
in your being
how lonesome
your life journey
has been so far
some life spaces are
so,so vacant
one was oblivious
till they get filled
inside out with
some soul's energy field
such cosmic occurrence
are momentous
and monumental as well
they metamorphose you.
some souls
fill in
your empty existence.

All My Life

All my life
I was restless
searching for the unknown
undefined, abstract existence
suddenly I feel so fulfilled
so complete
I surrender myself to life
knowing nothing
seeking nothing
not even you my soul
I am not craving for you
I am filled with you.

Forgetting

Forgetting
is an effort to
deny remembering
denials are not permanent
they come they go
they reinforce
all that is denied
forgetting is remembering
more than ever
some souls are omnipresent
in forgetting
In remembering.

Can Move Mountains

Can move mountains
cross seven seas
soul will do what it takes
to unite with its twin
to fulfil the purpose
universe celebrates awakening
miracle will happen
when it is to happen

Soul Songs

Soul songs
are never heard
words fail
they do not suffice
pure communication
melts in each pore of the skin
they reach the soul effortlessly
be quiet be calm
just travel inside your core
no noisy thoughts
soul mate
even empty my thoughts
now, only now you can
hear the soul song.

Touch It Once

*Touch it once
touch one life each day
touch with your smile
if you cannot do anything else
if you have nothing to offer
then smile from your heart
smile from your eyes
give a genuine smile
from the core of your existence
just give something
send a loving thought
touch a soul
from a distance of million miles
that is love
touch it once
touch one life each day.*

The Nip In The Air

*The nip in the air
has a soothing effect
just like your reassuring smile
vulnerable yet comforting
your telepathic thoughts
cross my mind
while I am walking with myself
you often join me
in my solitary journey
like an old forgotten song
like a childhood memory
like a morning dream
one remembers vividly
The nip in the air
has a soothing effect
just like your reassuring smile.*

After Crossing Seven Seas

After crossing seven oceans
and thousands of miles
You will touch
the moist morning soil of my city
the rising sun will
get a glimpse of you
my city will soak itself
with your presence
will transform and
never be
the same ever
though I shall
wait till eternity to see you
I will touch the moist morning soil of my city
try to feel the air
for your fragrance
look for your footprints
and write a poem on them
my words will linger forever
in the soul of my city
only you will
not be there to know
the longing of your twin soul.

Ends Are Beginnings 3

Ends are beginnings
Ends are
beginnings
an incessant process
universe destroys
and creates
transforms
form to formlessness
formlessness to form
tireless, endless cosmic dance
unknown and yet known
a miracle, energy field
our journey
from dust to dust
from nothing to nothing
part of the universe
also the universe we are
why rejoice the beginning
or lament the end
an incessant process
from dust to dust
from nothing to nothing
ends are
beginnings.

Sangeeta Gupta is a highly acclaimed artist, poet and documentary film maker. She served as a bureaucrat, an IRS Officer (**1984** batch). After a successful career in the Ministry of Finance, she retired as Chief Commissioner of Income Tax (May **2018**). She has also worked as Advisor (finance & administration) of Lalit Kala Akademi, National Akademi of Visual Arts (July **2019** to January **2020**). She is a member of the Finance Committee of Jawaharlal Nehru University since November **2018**.

She has to her credit **35** solo exhibitions of paintings, **20** published books and **9** of her poetry books are translated in several languages. She has directed, scripted and shot **8** documentary films which are in the collection of Library of Congress, U.S.A.
A film, **Life Beyond Tax**, has been made about her life by Tax India.

She is a bilingual poet and has twelve anthologies of poems in Hindi and three in English to her credit.
Antas Se (**1988**), a collection of Hindi Poems
Nagfani Ke Jungle (**1991**), a collection of Hindi short stories.
Iss Paar Uss Paar (**1996**), a book of her hand-written Hindi poems and drawings.
Samudra Se Lautati Nadi (**1999**), a collection of Hindi Poems
Pratinaad (**2005**), a book of Hindi poems and drawings/ paintings.
Lekhak Ka Samay (**2006**), a compilation of interviews taken by her of eminent women writers.
Weaves Of Time (**2013**), a collection of English poems.
Sparsh Ke Gulmohar(**2015**), a collection of Hindi poems.
Ladakh: Knowing the Unknown (**2015**), a book of rare photographs with poetic narrative.
Ekam (**2017**), a book of English poems with photographs of Dal Lake in different moods.
Song of Silence (**2018**), a collection of poems in English.
Beparwah Ruh (**2018**), a collection of Hindi poems

Mussavir ka Khayal (**2018**), a book of her hand-written poems and drawings.
Roshani Ka Safar (**2019**), a book of her hand-written poems and paintings.
Lal Butti Ke Bachhe (**2019**), a collection of Hindi poems
Beej sirf Zamin Par Ugate Hain(**2019**), a collection of Hindi poems
Ek Khwab Aasma Hua Jata Hai(**2019**), a collection of Hindi poems.
Jammu: Shades of Time (**2019**), a book of photographs with narrative about the scenic beauty and culture of Jammu.
Kashmir: Spirit of Solace (**2019**), a book of photographs with narrative about the scenic beauty and culture of Kashmir.
Song of the Cosmos (**2018**), is her creative biography as an artist, poet and film maker.

Her books of poems are translated in many languages, Greek, Mandarin, English, German, Bangla, Dogri and Urdu.

Selected Participation

2020: Weaves of Time, Song of Silence, both books are translated and published in Mandarin.

2020: Poetry reading in Afsarana Adab, online Art, culture and Literature festival, Jashne Adab.

2020: Part of the anthology of poetry, Lamakaan, edited by Anand Khatri, Poiesis Society For Poetry, Delhi.

2020: Poetry reading at Jashn-e-Hind, IGNCA, Delhi.

2019: Participated in Grand 'mushaira' in Oshawa, Toronto, Canada.

2019: Part of the anthology of poetry, Kavita Paraspar, published by Vijaya Books.

2019: Poems published in the anthology of **39**th world Congress Of Poets, SETU a bilingual journal, Pittsburgh, USA, Destine Literare, North America.
Poems are regularly published in Literary Vibes, Bhubhneshwar. Poems were adjudged as highly commended poems for both October and November **2019** by Destiny Poets

International Community of Poets (ICOP), Wakefield, U.K. Been adjudged as one of the Commended critics for December **2019**, by Destiny Poets International Community of Poets,(ICOP),Wakefield, U.K.

2019: National Academy Of Direct Taxes, Nagpur participating poet and Chief Guest at the closing ceremony of Literature Festival Anubhuti.

2019: Participated in **39**th World Congress of Poets held at Bhubneshwar, where three of her collection of poems were also launched.

2019: 'Arz Kia Hai' poetry reading at Prithvi Fine Arts and Cultural Centre, Delhi.

2019: Chief Guest and participating poet at **5**th Global Literary Festival, Noida.

2018: Poetry reading at Deccan Literature Festival, Pune.

2018: National Academy Of Direct Taxes, Nagpur participating poet and Chief Guest at the inaugural ceremony of Literature Festival Anubhuti.

2018: Poetry reading, Panelist at Valley Of Words Literature Festival, Dehradun.

2018: Mushayra Jashne Adab, Poetry festival, **2018**, Jamia Humdard, Delhi.

2018: Mushayra Jashne Adab, Poetry festival, **2018**, IGNCA, Delhi.

2017: Panel discussion, Jashne Adab, Poetry festival **2017** IGNCA, New Delhi,

2017: Khawateen Ka Mushaira, Jashne Adab, Poetry festival, IGNCA, Delhi and poetry reading in Art Gallery at CSOI, Delhi.

2017: Poetry reading organised by Sahitya Akademi, Delhi.

2017: Lekhak Se Rubaroo, Interviewed at **3**rd Global Literary Festival, Noida organized by ICMEI and Asian Academy Of Arts, Noida.

2017: Poetry reading at Kavi Sammelan-Mushaira organized by CSOI, Delhi.

2017: Inaugural address, poetry reading and panel discussion Anubhuti, a festival of art and literature at National Academy of Direct Taxes, Nagpur.

2017: Chief Editor of the In-house Magazine of Income Tax Department Delhi, Parikrama, Annual Issue. Layout and cover design of the magazine was also done by her.

2017: Pen and Brush, a session exploring the connection between colours and poetry organised by Oxford Book Store, Delhi.

 2017: Poetry reading and panel discussion on film making at Kalinga Literature Festival, Bhubaneswar.

2017: Sparsh Ke Gulmohar, collection of Hindi poems translated in Dogri ,launched at Jammu University, Jammu.

2017: EKAM a book of English poems with photographs of Dal Lake, launched at Jaipur Literature Festival.

2016: Chief Editor of the In-house Magazine of Income Tax Department, J&K Aaykar Shikhar, Annual Issue. Layout and cover design of the magazine was also done by her.

2016: Weaves of Time, collection of poems translated in Greek, launched in Greece.

2015: Ladakh: Knowing The Unknown (a book of rare photographs published by Full Circle **2015**) launched at Jaipur Literature Festival. The book was also launched by SKETBE, Thessaloniki, Nehru Centre, London and Ramada Hotel, Belfast, Northern Ireland.

2015: Sparsh Ke Gulmohar (collection of Hindi poems), launched at Delhi Film Festival.

2014: Participated in the panel discussion, Creative Pursuits of Civil Servants at Delhi Literature Festival, IGNCA, New Delhi.

2013: Weaves Of Time, collection of poems launched by Dr. Shashi Tharoor and Sh. Keshav Malik at India Habitat Centre, Delhi.

2013: Participated in World Hindi Conference organized by Srijangatha.com held at Thailand, Cambodia and Vietnam.

2012: Invited and sponsored by the Indian Council of Cultural Relations, Delhi for a rendition of her poems on the closing ceremony of the **9**th World Hindi Conference held at Johannesburg, South Africa.

2012: Invited by the Indian Society Of Authors in Collaboration with India International Centre, Delhi to speak about her creative process and read poems at India International Centre for their ongoing series "Who am I".

2012: Assistant Chief Editor of the In-house Magazine of Income Tax Department, Delhi, Parikrama, annual issue. Layout and cover design of the magazine was also done by her.

2011: Co-Editor – Celebration Through Art, a book launched on the eve of **150** years celebration of The Income Tax Department.

2009: Visions & Illumination, a book of poems by Keshav Malik along with her paintings.

2008: Whole issue was wholly dedicated to her writings and paintings (Issue **19**, January - April **2008**) of the magazine Punashch, edited by Dinesh Dwivedi, published from Madhya Pradesh.

2006: Lekhak Ka Samay, compilation of interviews taken by her, published and launched by Rajkamal Prakashan.
2005: Pratinaad (Book of Poems & Paintings-published in Hindi, translated in English, German & Bangla)
1999: Samudra Se Lautati Nadi, a collection of Hindi poems with her Ink drawings.
1998: Iss Paar Uss Paar (Bangla translation)
1996: Iss Paar Uss Paar (Hindi Poems), launched in Kolkata and Delhi.
1996-97: Editor - Women's Sahyog, annual issues.
1991: Nagfani Ke Jungle (Collection of Short Stories), published by Atul Prakashan, Allahabad.
1988: Antas Se (Hindi Poems), her first book, foreword written by legendary Hindi Poet Mahadevi Verma, published by Sahitya Bhawan Limited, Allahabad.

Her Paintings and Drawings are on book covers of several eminent writers.
Widely travelled, lives and works in Delhi, India.

Studio A-1/232, Safdarjung Enclave,
New Delhi- 110029, India
sangeetaguptaart@gmail.com
artsangeetagupta.com